KU-092-205

Gone Forever!
Woolly Mammoth

Rupert Matthews

www.heinemann.co.uk/library
Visit our website to find out more information about Heinemann Library books.

To order:

 Phone ++44 (0)1865 888066

Send a fax to ++44 (0)1865 314091

 Visit the Heinemann Bookshop at www.heinemann.co.uk/library to browse our catalogue and order online.

First published in Great Britain by Heinemann Library, Halley Court, Jordan Hill, Oxford OX2 8EJ, a part of Harcourt Education. Heinemann is a registered trademark of Harcourt Education Ltd.

© Harcourt Education Ltd 2003.
The moral right of the proprietor has been asserted.

All rights reserved. No part of this publication may be reproduced, stored in a retrieval system, or transmitted in any form or by any means, electronic, mechanical, photocopying, recording, or otherwise without either the prior written permission of the Publishers or a licence permitting restricted copying in the United Kingdom issued by the Copyright Licensing Agency Ltd, 90 Tottenham Court Road, London W1T 4LP (www.cla.co.uk).

Editorial: Andrew Farrow and Dan Nunn
Design: Ron Kamen and Paul Davies & Associates
Illustrations: Maureen and Gordon Gray, James Field (SGA) and Darren Lingard
Picture Research: Maria Joannou, Rebecca Sodergren and Frances Topp
Production: Viv Hichens
Originated by Ambassador Litho Ltd
Printed and bound in China by South China Printing Company

07 06 05 04 03
10 9 8 7 6 5 4 3 2 1
ISBN 0 431 16603 X

British Library Cataloguing in Publication Data
Matthews, Rupert
Woolly Mammoth - (Gone forever)
1. Woolly mammoth - Juvenile literature
I. Title
569.6'7

Acknowledgements

The Publishers are grateful to the following for permission to reproduce photographs: Ardea pp. **6** (Francois Gohier), **12** (Masahiro Iijuna), **22** (Peter Morris); Corbis p. **8**; Museum of Natural History, Vienna p. **24**; Natural History Museum, London pp. **14**, **18**; NHPA p. **4** (Roger Tidman), **20** (Stephen Kraseman); Novosti p. **16**; Scala Art Resource p. **10**; Science Photo Library p. **26**.

Cover photo reproduced with permission of The Natural History Museum, London.

Our thanks to Dr David Norman, Dr Angela Milner and Dr Andy Currant for their assistance in the preparation of this book.

Every effort has been made to contact copyright holders of any material reproduced in this book. Any omissions will be rectified in subsequent printings if notice is given to the Publishers.

Disclaimer

All the Internet addresses (URLs) given in this book were valid at the time of going to press. However, due to the dynamic nature of the Internet, some addresses may have changed, or sites may have ceased to exist since publication. While the author and publishers regret any inconvenience this may cause readers, no responsibility for any such changes can be accepted by either the author or the publishers.

-46650

649024   SCH

JS69

Contents

Some words are shown in bold, **like this**.
You can find out what they mean by looking in the Glossary.

Gone forever!

About 50,000 years ago Europe was much colder than it is today. Scientists call this time of very cold weather an **Ice Age**. Several types of animal lived during this Ice Age. Scientists have dug their **fossils** out of the ground.

One of the animals that lived during the Ice Age was the Woolly Mammoth. When warmer weather began about 10,000 years ago, the Woolly Mammoth became **extinct**. This means that all mammoths died.

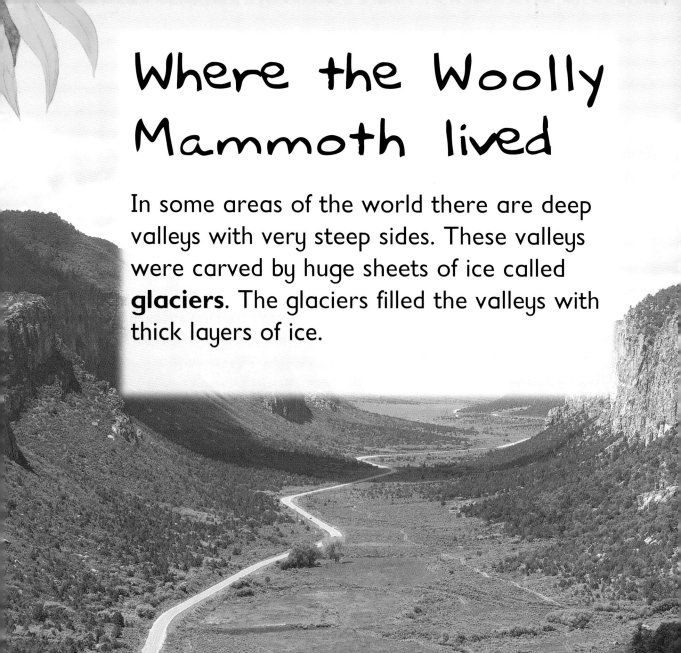

Where the Woolly Mammoth lived

In some areas of the world there are deep valleys with very steep sides. These valleys were carved by huge sheets of ice called **glaciers**. The glaciers filled the valleys with thick layers of ice.

Even where the land was not covered in solid ice, it was very cold. In places like this, it snowed for ten months of the year. During the other two months, some plants grew before it snowed again.

Plants of the Ice Age

Scientists can discover what plants grew 10,000 years ago by studying **peat bogs**. Peat bogs are areas of wet ground where **moss** grows in deep layers. Plant seeds were caught in the bogs and have been **preserved**.

At the time of the Woolly Mammoth, the plants in Europe could survive in the cold weather. These plants included short trees and shrubs, like the **birch**, **willow** and **heather**. Grasses covered the ground during the short summer.

9

Other animals

Several other types of animal lived in the **Ice Age** alongside the Woolly Mammoth. Humans also lived at this time. They painted pictures on cave walls that show some of these animals.

cave painting from Lascaux, in France

The **Woolly Rhinoceros** lived at the same time as the Woolly Mammoth. The rhinoceros was covered in fur to keep it warm. It had two horns, one of which was over one metre long. Like the Woolly Mammoth, this creature is now **extinct**.

What was the Woolly Mammoth?

Scientists have found the remains of mammoths frozen in the ground in Alaska and Siberia (in modern-day Russia). The ice has **preserved** their bodies. Scientists have studied these frozen mammoths to find out how they lived.

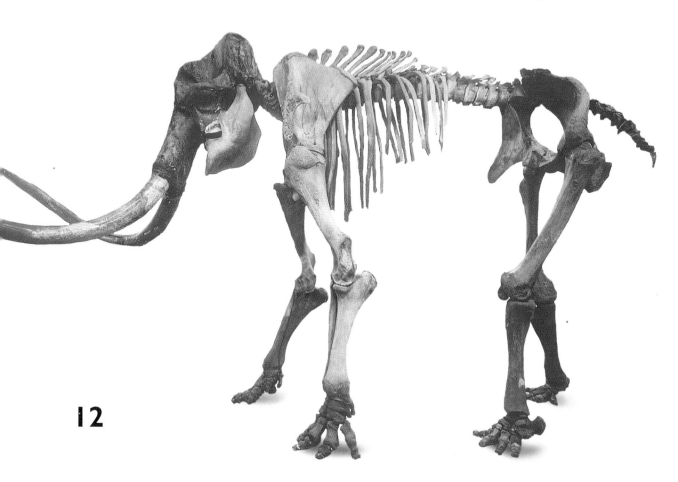

Woolly Mammoth was a type of elephant. It had a thick coat of fur to keep it warm. The animal also had thick layers of fat over its shoulders. These were like a store of food for the winter.

Baby mammoths

**remains
of a baby
mammoth**

Some scientists think that Woolly Mammoths may
have spent the winter in warmer lands to the south.
Babies would have been born in the spring when the
Woolly Mammoths moved back north again. The
babies took several years to grow into adults.

14

Young Woolly Mammoths were looked after by their mothers. For several years each youngster followed its mother. The mother showed it which plants were good to eat and how to shelter from the winter weather.

The woolly coat

Frozen mammoths have been found complete with their woolly **hides**. These show that the Woolly Mammoth had two types of fur. The outer hair was long and thick. The inner hair was soft and furry.

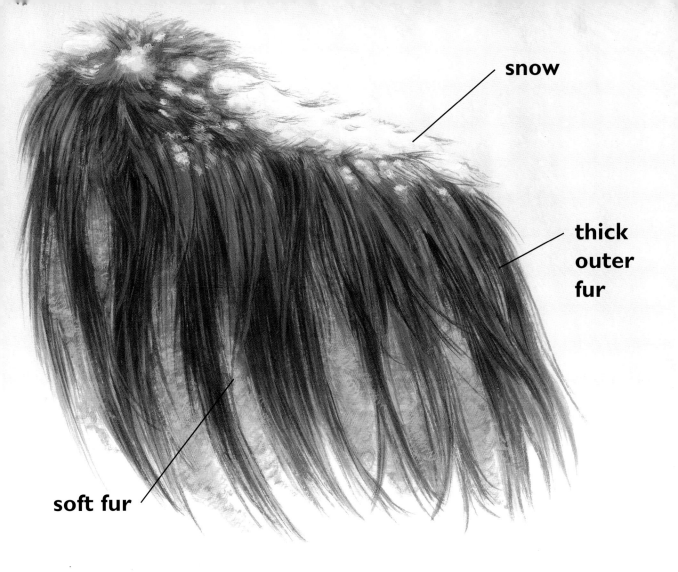

snow

thick
outer
fur

soft fur

The soft fur next to the skin kept the Woolly
Mammoth warm in the coldest weather. The thick
outer hair stopped snow or rain from reaching the
soft fur and making it damp and cold.

17

The mighty tusks

Woolly Mammoths had long, curved **tusks**.
Each tusk was over 3 metres long and weighed
about 130 kilograms. The tusks usually have many
short scratches on their undersides.

Woolly mammoths rubbed their tusks along the ground. They may have used them to push the snow off plants that they wished to eat.

A herd on the move

During the winter the land in the north became very cold. Deep snow covered the ground and there was nothing for Woolly Mammoths to eat. The Woolly Mammoths moved south to warmer areas.

Woolly Mammoths may have marched south in small **herds**. Each herd was probably led by the oldest female mammoth. When it got warmer, in the spring, the Woolly Mammoths moved north again.

Feast for a mammoth

The teeth of the Woolly Mammoth were large and strong. They had a surface made up of many sharp ridges. These ridges show that Woolly Mammoth ate tough plants like grasses or pine needles.

Woolly Mammoth tooth

ridges

The Woolly Mammoth used its trunk to pull grass from the ground or needles from pine trees. The mammoth's trunk put the food in its mouth. The teeth ground the plants before they were swallowed.

Lion attack!

The remains of large lions have been found in the same places as Woolly Mammoth remains. These lions had powerful claws and long, sharp teeth. They used these as weapons to attack their **prey**.

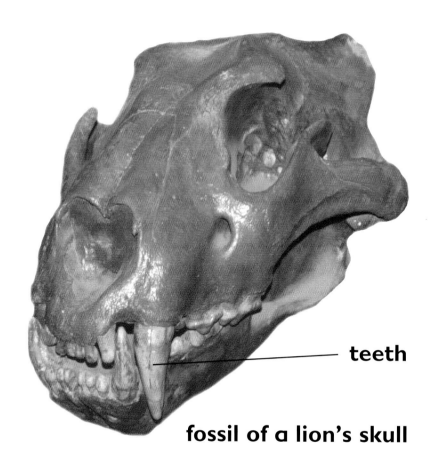

teeth

fossil of a lion's skull

Lions and other animals probably attacked young Woolly Mammoths. Adult Woolly Mammoths would have moved in front of the youngsters to protect them. If the attacker could not reach the young easily, it would give up and leave.

Hunted by humans

Scientists have found the remains of human campsites near where Woolly Mammoths lived. Hundreds of mammoth bones have been found at these sites. Woolly Mammoths were very useful to humans.

tent made of
Mammoth bones
and skin

Woolly
Mammoth
skin

Woolly
Mammoth
bones

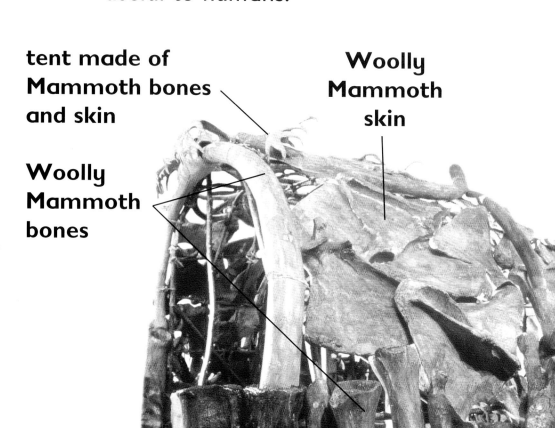

Humans ate the meat of Woolly Mammoths. They used the skins of Woolly Mammoths to make clothes and tents. They even built **huts** out of **tusks** and the long leg bones.

Woolly Mammoths around the world

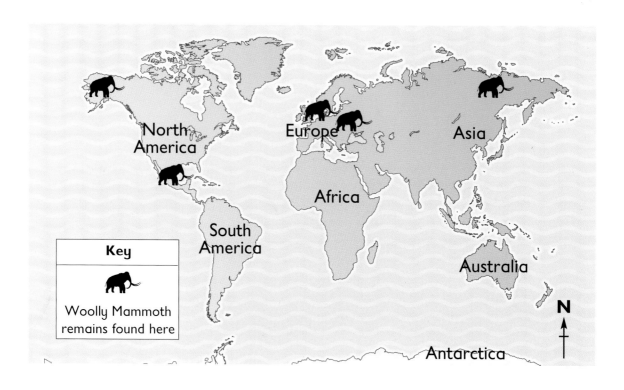

Woolly Mammoths lived across the northern lands of the world. Most Woolly Mammoths lived in northern Asia and Europe, but some lived in North America.

When did the Woolly Mammoth live?

Mammoths lived from about 3 million years ago (mya) to 4,500 years ago. This means they lived in the **Pliocene** and **Pleistocene Epochs** of the Age of Mammals.

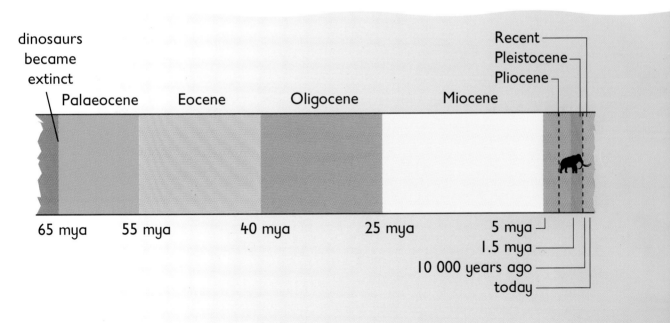

dinosaurs became extinct

Palaeocene Eocene Oligocene Miocene

Recent
Pleistocene
Pliocene

65 mya   55 mya   40 mya   25 mya   5 mya

1.5 mya

10 000 years ago

today

Fact file

Woolly Mammoth fact file	
Length:	3 metres
Weight:	up to 4.5 tonnes
Time:	Pliocene and Pleistocene Epochs, ending about 4,500 years ago.
Place:	Asia, Europe and North America

How to say it

mammoth – mamm-oth
Pleistocene – ply-stow-seen
rhinoceros – ry-nos-er-os

Glossary

birch short tree with white bark that can grow in places where the weather is very cold

epoch used to describe a certain period of time a long time ago

extinct an animal is extinct when there are none of its kind left alive

fossil remains of a plant or animal, usually found in rocks

glacier huge sheet of ice that moves slowly down a valley. Glaciers carve deep u-shaped valleys as they move.

heather woody bush with purple flowers

herd group of plant-eating animals that live together

hide animal's skin

hut temporary house built of wood, bones, animals skins or other materials

Ice Age very cold period of time. An Ice Age lasts hundreds of thousands of years.

moss small green plant that looks a bit like a carpet

peat bog very damp ground where thick layers of peat moss grow

Pleistocene period of time that began about 1.5 million years ago and ended about 10,000 years ago

Pliocene period of time that began about 5 million years ago and ended about 1.5 million years ago

preserve make something last a long time

prey animal hunted for food

tusk very long tooth

willow tree with narrow leaves, often found near water

Woolly Rhinoceros type of rhinoceros with dense fur. It is now extinct.

Find out more

These are some books about Woolly Mammoths:
A Woolly Mammoth Journey, Debbie Miller (Little Brown & Co., 2001)
Extinct: The Woolly Mammoth, Simon Furman (Channel 4 Books, 2001)
Woolly Mammoth: Life, Death and Rediscovery, Windsor Chorlton
    (Scholastic Reference, 2001)

Look at these websites for more information:
www.enchantedlearning.com/subjects/dinos
www.enchantedlearning.com/subjects/mammals
www.allaboutmammals.com/subjects/mammals/mammoth

Index

Titles in the *Gone Forever* series include:

Hardback   0 431 16604 8

Hardback   0 431 16602 1

Hardback   0 431 16605 6

Hardback   0 431 16601 3

Hardback   0 431 16600 5

Hardback   0 431 16603 X

Find out about the other titles in this series on our website www.heinemann.co.uk/library